The Story of Flight

AMAZING FLIGHTS

The Golden Age

Crabtree Publishing Company
www.crabtreebooks.com

PMB 16A, 350 Fifth Avenue
Suite 3308
New York, NY 10118

612 Welland Avenue
St. Catharines, Ontario
L2M 5V6

Published in 2003 by
Crabtree Publishing Company

Coordinating editor: Ellen Rodger
Project editors: Sean Charlebois, Carrie Gleason
Production coordinator: Rose Gowsell

Created and Produced by
David West 🏃 Children's Books

Project Development, Design, and Concept
David West Children's Books:
Designer: Rob Shone
Editor: James Pickering
Illustrators: Neil Reed & Hemesh Alles (Allied Artists),
James Field & Ross Watton (SGA), Colin Howard
(Advocate), Alex Pang
Picture Research: Carlotta Cooper

Photo Credits:
Abbreviations: t-top, m-middle, b-bottom, r-right,
l-left, c-center.

Front cover tm & pages 17br - Rex Features Ltd. 4tr,
6tl, 10bl, 15br, 26tl - Castrol. 5tl (PC 72/110/35),
6bl (P11384), 8tl (PC 74/41/428), 11tr, 12tl (4728-
2), 13tr (4728-5), 15tr (PC 74/4/53), 18tl (PC
74/41/426) & bl (PC 74/ 41/ 353), 20ml (5603-3),
22tl (5651-7), 24tl (P1201) & bl (P6563), 27tl (AC
72/25/100), 28tl, 29br (5873-4) - Royal Air Force
Museum. 17tr, 23tr - Hulton Archive. 20tl - The
Flight Collection

06 05 04 03

10 9 8 7 6 5 4 3 2 1

Printed and bound in Dubai

Cataloging in Publication Data
Hansen, Ole Steen.
   Amazing flights--the golden age / Ole Steen Hansen.
    p. cm. -- (The story of flight)
Includes index.
ISBN 0-7787-1202-8 (RLB) -- ISBN 0-7787-1218-4 (PB)
   1. Aeronautics--History--Juvenile literature. 2. Flight--History--
Juvenile literature. [1. Aeronautics--History. 2. Flight--History.]
I. Title. II. Series.
   TL515.H255 2003
   629.13'09--dc21
                                                    2002156479
                                                         LC

The Story of Flight

AMAZING FLIGHTS
The Golden Age

Ole Steen Hansen

 Crabtree Publishing Company
www.crabtreebooks.com

CONTENTS

HIGH ACHIEVERS
Aviators were treated as heroes between the World Wars, and people crowded to see them in air races and at airshows. The 1934 Castrol Year Book (below) charted their achievements.

INTRODUCTION

Immediately after World War I, aviators set out to prove that airplanes could reach every corner of the globe. The two decades between the wars are known as "the golden age of flight." People admired the pilots, and the press loved to write about them as much as they do about pop or sports stars today. Record-breaking pilots were greeted by large cheering crowds when they arrived at their destinations. They were introduced to presidents and kings. Others never made it and simply disappeared. The last anybody saw of them was at take-off, their airplane fading to a tiny speck in the sky with the still more distant roar of the engine.

DOWN TO EARTH

Long journeys by air were very risky. The first non-stop flight across the Atlantic ended in a crash, but at least this crew made it across "the pond," as the ocean is often called.

SMALL PLANE, BIG SKY

Long distance flying meant hours in tiny cockpits behind noisy engines. In 1931, a Lockheed Vega plane named *Winnie Mae* flew around the world in a record time of 8 days, 15 hours, and 52 minutes.

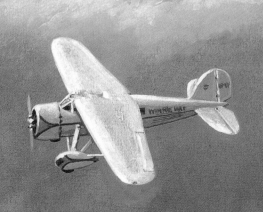

ACROSS THE ATLANTIC

TAKING OFF
John Alcock and Arthur Brown, like other long-distance flyers, faced the difficulty of taking off in an underpowered aircraft that was heavy with fuel.

Between May and July 1919, the Atlantic Ocean was crossed by two airplanes and one airship. These were the first non-stop and return flights across the ocean. It had only been ten years since the first flight across the English Channel had made headlines.

On June 14, John Alcock and Arthur Whitten Brown took off in their Vickers Vimy plane from Newfoundland, off the coast of Canada. The Vimy was a World War I **bomber** which had been modified to fly the long distance.

R-34
The British airship R-34 made the first two-way crossing of the Atlantic. Against strong **headwinds**, it was flown from Scotland to New York in four and a half days, which was only slightly better than the fastest steam ships of the day. The return journey to England lasted three days and three hours.

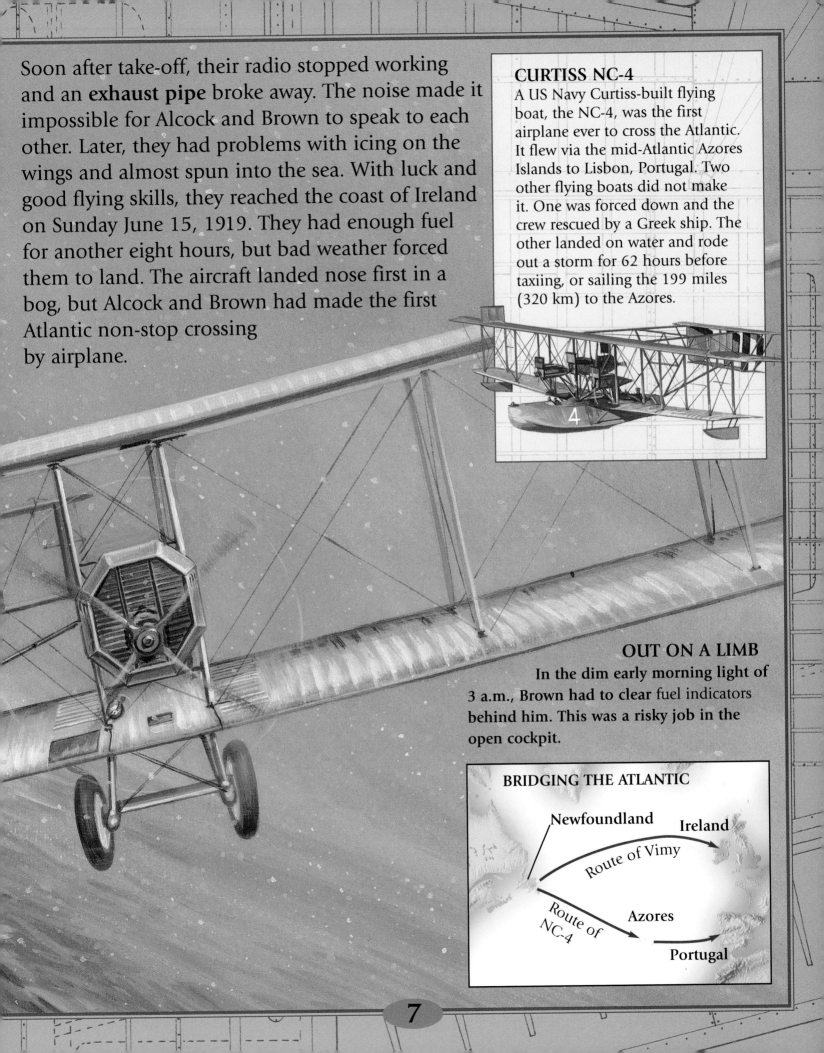

Soon after take-off, their radio stopped working and an **exhaust pipe** broke away. The noise made it impossible for Alcock and Brown to speak to each other. Later, they had problems with icing on the wings and almost spun into the sea. With luck and good flying skills, they reached the coast of Ireland on Sunday June 15, 1919. They had enough fuel for another eight hours, but bad weather forced them to land. The aircraft landed nose first in a bog, but Alcock and Brown had made the first Atlantic non-stop crossing by airplane.

CURTISS NC-4

A US Navy Curtiss-built flying boat, the NC-4, was the first airplane ever to cross the Atlantic. It flew via the mid-Atlantic Azores Islands to Lisbon, Portugal. Two other flying boats did not make it. One was forced down and the crew rescued by a Greek ship. The other landed on water and rode out a storm for 62 hours before taxiing, or sailing the 199 miles (320 km) to the Azores.

OUT ON A LIMB

In the dim early morning light of 3 a.m., Brown had to clear fuel indicators behind him. This was a risky job in the open cockpit.

BRIDGING THE ATLANTIC

Newfoundland   Ireland

Route of Vimy

Route of NC-4   Azores

Portugal

BARNSTORMERS

All over the USA, pilots went barnstorming in the 1920s. They landed in fields near small towns and often slept under their wings at night. Most barely made a living, but they were flying!

ALAN COBHAM

Cobham was one of the great pilots between the World Wars. He was a test pilot, long distance flyer, organizer of a flying circus, and pioneer of in-flight refueling.

When World War I ended in 1918, thousands of ex-air force pilots found themselves without a job. They wanted to fly, but could not afford to do it for fun, and the new airlines that were starting up only employed a few of them. Barnstorming became the answer. In cheap **surplus** training aircraft, such as Curtiss Jennies and DH 4 bombers, they traveled from town to town. They performed daredevil stunts in the air and sold joyrides to millions of people. In Britain, Alan Cobham's Flying Circus toured the country in the 1930s. One pilot became famous for using his wingtip to pick up a handkerchief which a lady had "accidentally" dropped.

Bessie Coleman

Bessie Coleman wanted to fly, but no American flying school of the time would teach an African-American woman. She learned to fly in France and went back to the United States as a stunt flyer. She demanded that all people be admitted through the same gate at her shows. Her dream of setting up a flying school that accepted African-Americans was never fulfilled, because she was killed in a flying accident.

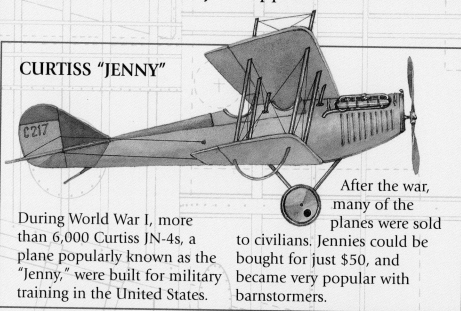

CURTISS "JENNY"

During World War I, more than 6,000 Curtiss JN-4s, a plane popularly known as the "Jenny," were built for military training in the United States. After the war, many of the planes were sold to civilians. Jennies could be bought for just $50, and became very popular with barnstormers.

DEATH DEFYING
Barnstormers and pilots working for the movie industry took great risks. Their stunts included hanging from a plane by their teeth, and climbing from one plane to another, or from a car to an airplane.

FLYING OVER FUJI
"Grandiose in its beauty" was how the pilot described the view of Mount Fuji.

TO INDIA
Mary du Caurroy, an English **noblewoman**, made her first flight in 1926 when she was 61 years old. She was fascinated by flying, and in 1929 hired a pilot to help her make a record-breaking flight from England to India and back in a Fokker F. VII-3m plane. She later learned to fly herself, but disappeared on a solo flight in 1937.

ACROSS ASIA

In 1926, two Danish military aviators, Captain Botved and Aircraftman Olsen, made one of the first flights between Europe and Japan. It lasted three months and they faced many problems on their way. Another aircraft with them crashed in India. Botved and Olsen made it all the way from Copenhagen, in Denmark, to Tokyo, in Japan, and back.

At the time, not many people traveled far, even within their own country. A flight across Asia was a big deal in the 1920s, and the pilots were treated like heroes everywhere they landed. Over China, a fuel tank leaked and their plane was forced to land on a 650-foot long (200-m) piece of land between the thousands of small flooded rice fields. Botved and Olsen had to walk a long way to find fuel. When they finally got back to the plane, some of the nuts, bolts, and spare parts were missing. Early long distance flyers faced the danger of being stranded in remote areas.

FOKKER CV

Botved and Olsen flew one of the most modern military aircraft of the time, a Fokker CV. During World War I, Dutch aircraft designer Anthony Fokker had started to develop thick, strong wings that did not need to be supported by wires. The Fokker CV was an open biplane, and the wings were not wire braced.

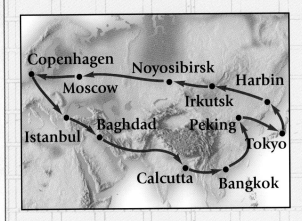

THERE AND BACK

Botved and Olsen landed 47 times on their way to Japan. They flew a route over Eastern Europe, the Middle East, India, Southeast Asia, and China. Flying back from Japan, they landed 16 times on the relatively unknown route over Russia and the vast Siberian forests. They spent a total of 193 hours and 15 minutes in the air.

LINDBERGH

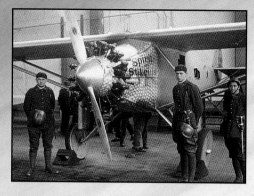

Charles Lindbergh was the first person to fly across the Atlantic Ocean solo. His flight was the first non-stop flight from North America to the European mainland. Lindbergh's flight created an enormous interest in aviation.

THE WORLD'S MOST FAMOUS PLANE

The *Spirit of St Louis* landed in Paris. After returning to the United States on a ship, Lindbergh toured North and South America in the plane. In 1928, he presented it to the Smithsonian Institution.

Lindbergh was an experienced airmail pilot when he decided to fly solo across the Atlantic. St Louis businessmen paid for his Ryan aircraft and Lindbergh named it *Spirit of St Louis*. Heavy with fuel, he barely cleared the telephone lines at the end of the runway when he took off. Staying awake was the main problem during the 33-hour flight. He often had to put his face out into the **slipstream** through the side window to keep himself awake. Once during the flight, Lindbergh, half asleep, almost crashed his plane into the sea. In the end he reached Paris, where wild and happy crowds jumped the airport fence and rushed up to his plane.

LAND

It was a great relief for pilots to see land after long hours over the sea. Not every pilot made it. French pilot Charles Nungesser disappeared without a trace over the Atlantic Ocean just two weeks before Lindbergh made his famous flight.

1 Skylight
2 Wicker chair
3 Engine throttle
4 Control stick
5 Periscope
6 Main fuel tank
7 Oil and fuel gauges
8 Altimeter
9 Air speed indicator

Légion d'Honneur

Lindbergh, or "lucky Lindy" as he became known, received several decorations for his epic flight. In France, he was awarded the country's highest honor, the *Légion d'Honneur*. A French general said: "Not only have you united two continents, but also the hearts of people everywhere, in admiration for the simple courage of a man who accomplished a great thing."

IN THE DRIVING SEAT

The *Spirit of St Louis* had very basic instruments compared to modern aircraft. A large 450-gallon (1,705-L) fuel tank was mounted in front of the pilot under the wing. With the tank in this position, the **center of gravity** would not change when the fuel burned. The tank made it hard for Lindbergh to see straight ahead, so he had to use a **periscope** to see.

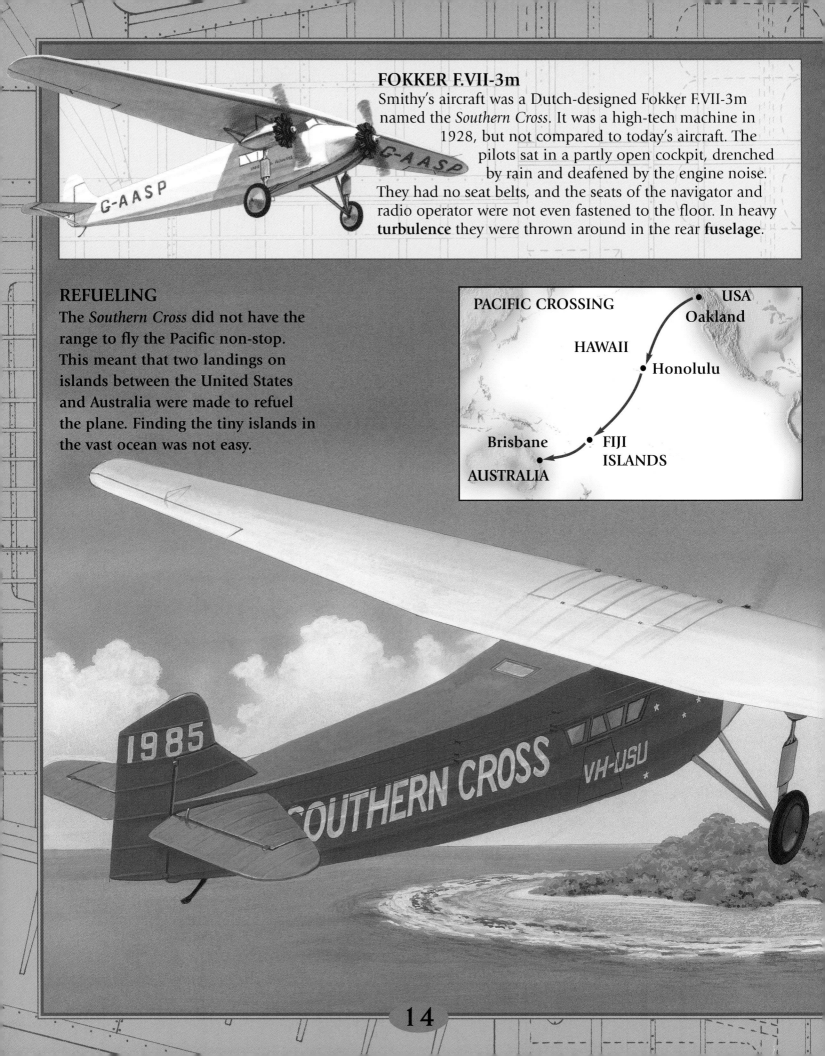

FOKKER F.VII-3m
Smithy's aircraft was a Dutch-designed Fokker F.VII-3m named the *Southern Cross*. It was a high-tech machine in 1928, but not compared to today's aircraft. The pilots sat in a partly open cockpit, drenched by rain and deafened by the engine noise. They had no seat belts, and the seats of the navigator and radio operator were not even fastened to the floor. In heavy **turbulence** they were thrown around in the rear **fuselage**.

REFUELING
The *Southern Cross* did not have the range to fly the Pacific non-stop. This meant that two landings on islands between the United States and Australia were made to refuel the plane. Finding the tiny islands in the vast ocean was not easy.

PACIFIC CROSSING

USA
Oakland
HAWAII
Honolulu
Brisbane
FIJI
ISLANDS
AUSTRALIA

THE SOUTHERN CROSS

The first flight across the Pacific was a dangerous journey. In 1928, Charles Kingsford Smith, known as "Smithy," and his crew flew the longest sea crossing at the time.

During the flight, the aviators saw only two ships, both at night and near Hawaii. Sometimes, navigation was impossible for hours on end, as the aircraft was tossed wildly in black threatening clouds. The last leg from Fiji was the worst. Smithy later remembered: "Rain, rain, rain! How sick we were of the rain. Lightning added fresh terrors to the night. We plunged on with no idea of where we were." Thanks to expert navigation, they reached the Australian coast 108 miles (175 km) south of Brisbane. It had taken 83 hours flying to cross the Pacific. Deafened, exhausted, but happy, the four aviators watched the local police hold back the cheering crowds as they shut down their engines.

LAST FLIGHT
Smithy broke more records with the *Southern Cross*. To make money, he also gave many people their first flights, joyriding in the famous plane. In 1935, he disappeared off Burma, in Southeast Asia, on a long distance flight.

Bert Hinkler
Bert Hinkler was an Australian who had served with the Royal Flying Corps during World War I. After the war he became a famous test pilot and long distance flyer. His greatest feat was a record-breaking solo flight from England to Australia in 1928.

A LOVE OF THE SAHARA

Despite the dangers, Saint-Exupéry loved the desert landscape, especially when spending the night in the open, with just the wind, the sand, and the countless stars in the dark sky above him.

THE MAIL CARRIERS

Flying airmail helped early American airlines survive financially. From 1926, the Douglas M-2 was used by the Western Air Service on the Los Angeles to Salt Lake City run. Occasionally, passengers were flown in the mail compartment in front of the pilot, where 900 lbs (450 kg) of mail and parcels were also carried.

DESERT MAIL

French pilots were the first to fly airmail routes over the western Sahara to Dakar, in Africa. From here, the mail was sailed to South America. Later, the mail was flown all the way across the South Atlantic, too.

Flights across the desert were dangerous. Even if an emergency landing was successful, the pilot had to fix his engine before heat and thirst killed him. Other dangers were local people who shot at mail planes. French pilot Antoine de Saint-Exupéry was working at a landing strip at Cape Judy in the Western Sahara in July 1928 when a plane went down in the desert because of engine failure. Saint-Exupéry set out with a mechanic and 15 armed guards to rescue the plane. They used six horses, two donkeys, a pack-camel, and two camels pulling a makeshift wheeled cart to carry the spare engine. While the mechanic changed the engine, the guards leveled out a 295-foot (90-m) runway between the sand dunes. In the afternoon, Saint-Exupéry flew the repaired aircraft back to the landing strip. Saint-Exupéry helped expand the airmail route and develop better relations between the local people and the French airmail company. He went missing during a flight in North Africa in World War II.

ANTOINE DE SAINT-EXUPÉRY

Saint-Exupéry (right) was not only famous as an airmail pilot, but was also a well-known writer. Saint-Exupéry's fairy tale *The Little Prince* was inspired by some of his forced landings in the desert.

Lindbergh

Charles Lindbergh flew airmail before setting out on his epic flight from New York to Paris. Airmail was flown in all kinds of weather, which taught Lindbergh a lot about handling airplanes in difficult conditions. Sometimes he had to parachute from the mailplane, because bad weather or technical trouble made it impossible to continue.

OVER THE POLES

COMMANDER BYRD

U.S. Navy Lieutenant-Commander Richard E. Byrd was the first person to fly over both the North and South Poles.

The first flights over the Poles meant flying in cold, unheated aircraft which was anything but comfortable. In the event of an emergency landing there was absolutely nobody to help the crew.

American Commander Richard Byrd helped plan the first flight over the Atlantic Ocean in 1919. He was very disappointed when he was not allowed to take part.

Then, on May 9, 1926, along with his pilot Floyd Bennett, he became the first man to fly over the North Pole.

The Norge

In 1925, Norwegian explorer Roald Amundsen made his first unsuccessful attempt to fly over the North Pole with two flying boats. In 1926 he succeeded with the airship *Norge*, but Byrd had already been over the Pole with his Fokker two days before. Amundsen flew the airship on to Alaska, completing the first Arctic flight between Europe and North America. The *Norge* was damaged during landing and could not be saved.

Byrd took off with his crew in their Fokker VII-3m plane from a bumpy snow runway on the Norwegian Island of Spitzbergen, about 745 miles (1,200 km) from the North Pole. The 16-hour flight went as planned, except for an oil leak. Then, in 1929 Byrd flew over the South Pole, where mountains reach up to 9,186 feet (2,800 m) high, making the flight a difficult one.

SPONSORS

Byrd had good sponsors for his Arctic flight. One was Edsel Ford (son of Henry Ford). Byrd named his aircraft *Josephine*, after Edsel's daughter.

FORD TRI-MOTOR

The Ford Tri-motor, or "Tin Goose," was used for everything, including flying passengers and cargo, fighting fires, and low level aerobatics. Byrd used this three-engine plane for his South Pole flight. His Tri-motor was so heavy that the supplies were thrown out to lighten the aircraft. The plane then managed to climb over the mountains with just 19 feet (6 m) to spare.

THE GREAT AIR RACE

ONLY JUST READY
The de Havilland Comet won the MacRobertson Air Race. It was developed in secret and test flown just six weeks before the race. It was fueled at Mildenhall before the race.

In the Stone Age, people used the same tools for thousands of years. In the twentieth century, things developed much faster. Aircraft raced half way around the world just 31 years after the Wright brothers had made their very first powered flight in 1903.

Jacqueline Cochran
American pilot Jacqueline Cochran entered the 1934 MacRobertson Air Race, but technical problems forced her to drop out in Romania. She achieved great fame for her later adventures in the air. In 1938, she won the Bendix Trophy in an air race. After World War II she became the first woman to break the sound barrier and also flew the Mach 2 Lockheed F-104 Starfighter. She held more speed, altitude, and distance records than any other pilot.

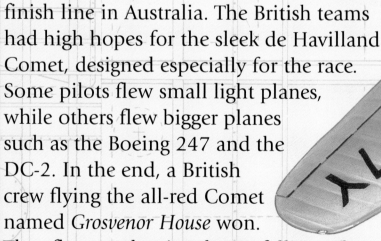

On October 20, 1934, the 20 contestants taking part in the MacRobertson Air Race took off from Mildenhall, England for the long flight to the finish line in Australia. The British teams had high hopes for the sleek de Havilland Comet, designed especially for the race. Some pilots flew small light planes, while others flew bigger planes such as the Boeing 247 and the DC-2. In the end, a British crew flying the all-red Comet named *Grosvenor House* won. They flew on despite almost falling asleep from fatigue. After 71 hours and 18 minutes they came in low and fast between the pylons at the Flemington Racecourse, in Melbourne, Australia.

DOUGLAS DC-2
Length: 62 ft (18.9 m)
Wingspan: 85 ft (25.9 m)
Speed: 191 mph (316 km/h)

RACE ROUTE

Mildenhall
Baghdad
Allahabad
Singapore
Charleville
Melbourne

BOEING 247D
Length: 51 ft 7 in (15.7 m)
Wingspan: 74 ft (22.5 m)
Speed: 189 mph (304 km/h)

DE HAVILLAND DH 88 COMET
Length: 29 ft (8.8 m)
Wingspan: 44 ft (13.4 m)
Speed: 237 mph (379 km/h)

DOUGLAS DC-2

The top American plane was the Douglas DC-2, which finished second in the race. It was a long range racer that could be used for little else. The DC-2 was a commercial airliner just off the assembly line, flown with more stops than necessary to promote the Dutch airline KLM and the idea of commercial air travel. Airlines around the world were very impressed with this aircraft.

Cockpit   Passenger area   Toilets   Cargo area

Pressurized Suits

Human beings cannot survive in low **air pressure** at very high altitude. When a British pilot flew a Bristol 138A to 50,000 feet (15,223 m) in 1936 he had to wear a pressure suit. On the way down he ran out of oxygen and had to smash the glass in his helmet in order to breathe.

PHOTOGRAPHING EVEREST

It took special equipment to fly over Mount Everest. The pilots wore oxygen masks to breathe. To survive in the extreme cold over the mountain they used electrically heated clothing – even their goggles were heated. Twice they flew over and photographed Everest, looking down on a landscape no one had ever seen before.

G-ACAZ

FLYING HIGH

In April 1933, two British Westland PV.3 planes flew over Mount Everest. This was not a world altitude record, but it was the first time the world's highest mountain had been flown over. If the plane ran into trouble, it could not make an emergency landing on the mountains, and the pilots would not survive.

Flying high was dangerous. In 1920, U.S. Major Rudolph W. Schroeder was nearly killed during a high altitude flight. His oxygen supply failed and he blacked out from lack of oxygen and exhaust fumes. He realized his problem, shut down his engine, and put the nose of the aircraft into a dive before passing out. He woke up and regained control at a lower altitude. On the first Everest flight, the photographer stepped on his own oxygen feed pipe. He repaired the fracture with his handkerchief.

JOHN MacREADY
In the early 1920s, American aviator John MacReady climbed higher than 32,808 feet (10,000 m) in his open cockpit biplane. It was a very cold experience.

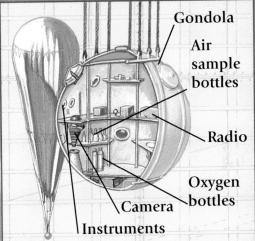

Gondola

Air sample bottles

Radio

Oxygen bottles

Camera

Instruments

HIGH ALTITUDE BALLOONS
In the early 1930s, the twin brothers Auguste and Jean Piccard flew balloons to altitudes higher than 49,213 feet (15,000 m), higher than any airplanes at the time. Their research helped in the development of pressurized cabins and oxygen supplies for high flying aircraft, and later for spacecraft, too.

SPEED

Between the World Wars, the world speed record went from 170 miles per hour (275 km/h) in 1920 to 469 miles per hour (755 km/h) in April 1939. The record breakers were highly specialized aircraft built only for the purpose of flying faster.

High-speed aircraft were built for winning prestigious trophies. The seaplanes competing for the Schneider Trophy were faster than military aircraft at the time. In 1932, American pilot Jimmy Doolittle won the Thompson Trophy.

THE SCHNEIDER TROPHY

Small seaplanes competed for the Schneider Trophy from 1911 to 1931. The trophy was finally won by Britain in a Supermarine S.6B.

HOWARD HUGHES H-1 RACER

Length: 26 ft 7 in (8.2 m)
Wingspan: 24 ft 6 in (7.6 m)
Speed: 345 mph (555 km/h)

Jimmy Doolittle

James Harold Doolittle was a pilot of exceptional skill. In 1922, he was the first pilot to cross the United States in less than 24 hours. In 1925, he won the Schneider Trophy race with his seaplane. During World War II he led the first air raid on Tokyo after the Pearl Harbor attack.

MACCHI MC72

Length: 27 ft 3 in (8.3 m)
Wingspan: 31 ft (9.5 m)
Speed: 440 mph (709 km/h)

This prize was awarded for speed at the National Air Races in the United States. Doolittle's Gee Bee R-1 was a dangerous aircraft to fly. His wife and son watched the air race closely, and they were in turn followed closely by photographers and journalists eager to record their reactions if Doolittle crashed! Luckily, he did not, but he never participated in the races again.

GEE BEE RACER MODEL R-1 SUPER SPORTSTER
Length: 17 ft 9 in (5.4 m)
Wingspan: 25 ft (7.6 m)
Speed: 300 mph (472 km/h)

SUPERMARINE S.6B
Length: 28 ft 10 in (8.8 m)
Wingspan: 30 ft (9.1 m)
Speed: 380 mph
(610 km/h)

ROLLS-ROYCE R-1 ENGINE
High speed aircraft gave designers important experience which was later used in the design of military aircraft. The Rolls-Royce engine on the Supermarine S.6B produced an amazing 2,350 horsepower (hp) but wore out in a few hours. Rolls-Royce used the technical knowledge gained from developing the engine to produce the Merlin, which was the engine that powered Spitfires and Hurricanes during the Battle of Britain in World War II.

FAMOUS AIRWOMEN

From the beginning of powered flight, most pilots were men. Between the World Wars, women wanted to fly too. Some became famous and admired long distance pilots.

Amy Johnson worked as a secretary in London, and she saved her money to pay for flying lessons. She became Britain's first licensed female aircraft mechanic. In 1930, she made the first female solo flight between England and Australia, and instantly became a celebrity.

SYDNEY HARBOR
To celebrate her achievement, Amy Johnson was flown over Sydney Harbor in a three-engined Fokker.

JASON
The Gipsy Moth airplane Amy Johnson used for her flight to Australia was named *Jason* after her father's business. He had paid for half of the plane. Her parents also insisted the seat be modified, so she could wear a parachute in it.

G-AARY

Jean Batten

New Zealander Jean Batten wanted fame as much as flying. Her first attempts at long distance flying were dangerous, but soon she became a very good pilot and navigator. Her flying skills saved her life during some very dangerous flights. She was always welcomed back in New Zealand by large crowds. After the first solo flight from Britain in 1936, a gathering of 6,000 people greeted her (left).

Amy Johnson made more record-breaking flights, and during World War II she flew aircraft from the factories to the squadrons. America's leading airwoman was Amelia Earhart. As a passenger, she became the first woman to fly across the Atlantic in 1928. She wanted to be at the controls though, and four years later she flew the Atlantic solo in her bright red Lockheed Vega.

FLYING FOR ALL

The de Havilland Gipsy Moth was used by both Amy Johnson and Jean Batten for their first long distance flights. It was a very popular plane with flying clubs, though not ideal for long flights. The two women used it because it was affordable!

AMELIA EARHART

Amelia Earhart set several records including an altitude record of 18,415 feet (5,613 m) for autogiros, and the first solo flight ever from Hawaii to the United States mainland. In 1937, during a flight around the world, she disappeared over the Pacific. Her intention had been to land and refuel on the tiny Howland Island, but she did not find it. Her last message over the radio was "position doubtful."

AROUND THE WORLD

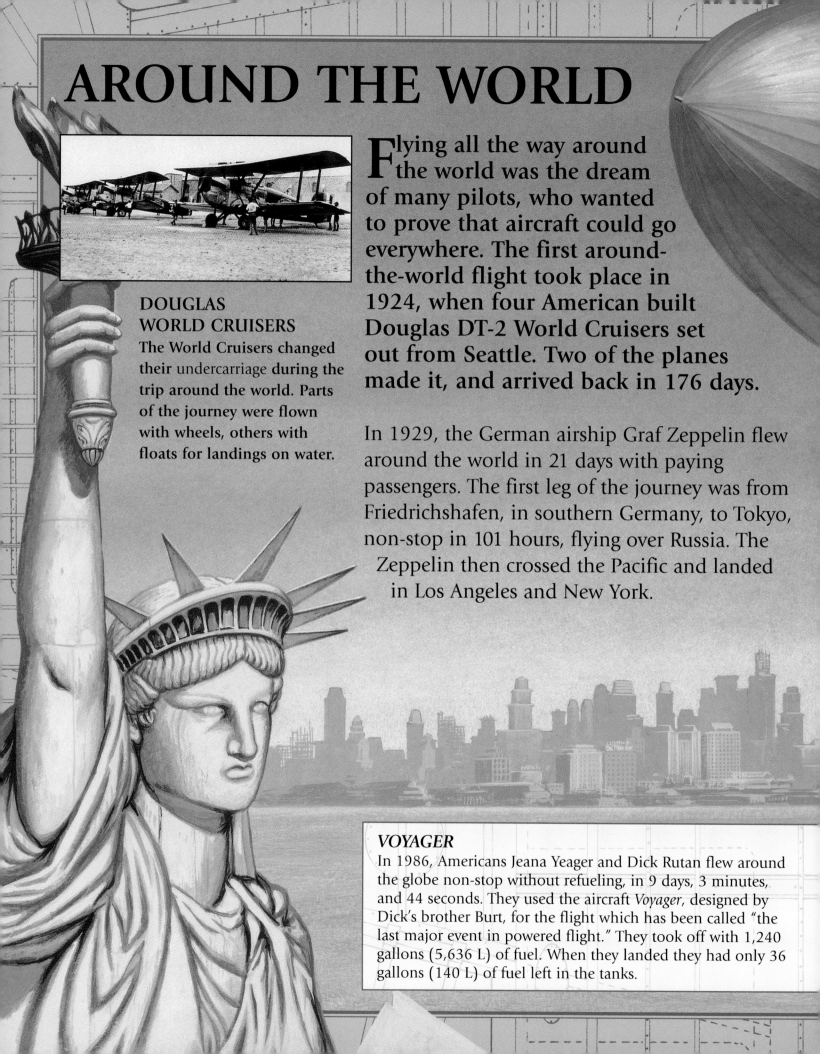

F lying all the way around the world was the dream of many pilots, who wanted to prove that aircraft could go everywhere. The first around-the-world flight took place in 1924, when four American built Douglas DT-2 World Cruisers set out from Seattle. Two of the planes made it, and arrived back in 176 days.

DOUGLAS WORLD CRUISERS

The World Cruisers changed their undercarriage during the trip around the world. Parts of the journey were flown with wheels, others with floats for landings on water.

In 1929, the German airship Graf Zeppelin flew around the world in 21 days with paying passengers. The first leg of the journey was from Friedrichshafen, in southern Germany, to Tokyo, non-stop in 101 hours, flying over Russia. The Zeppelin then crossed the Pacific and landed in Los Angeles and New York.

VOYAGER

In 1986, Americans Jeana Yeager and Dick Rutan flew around the globe non-stop without refueling, in 9 days, 3 minutes, and 44 seconds. They used the aircraft *Voyager*, designed by Dick's brother Burt, for the flight which has been called "the last major event in powered flight." They took off with 1,240 gallons (5,636 L) of fuel. When they landed they had only 36 gallons (140 L) of fuel left in the tanks.

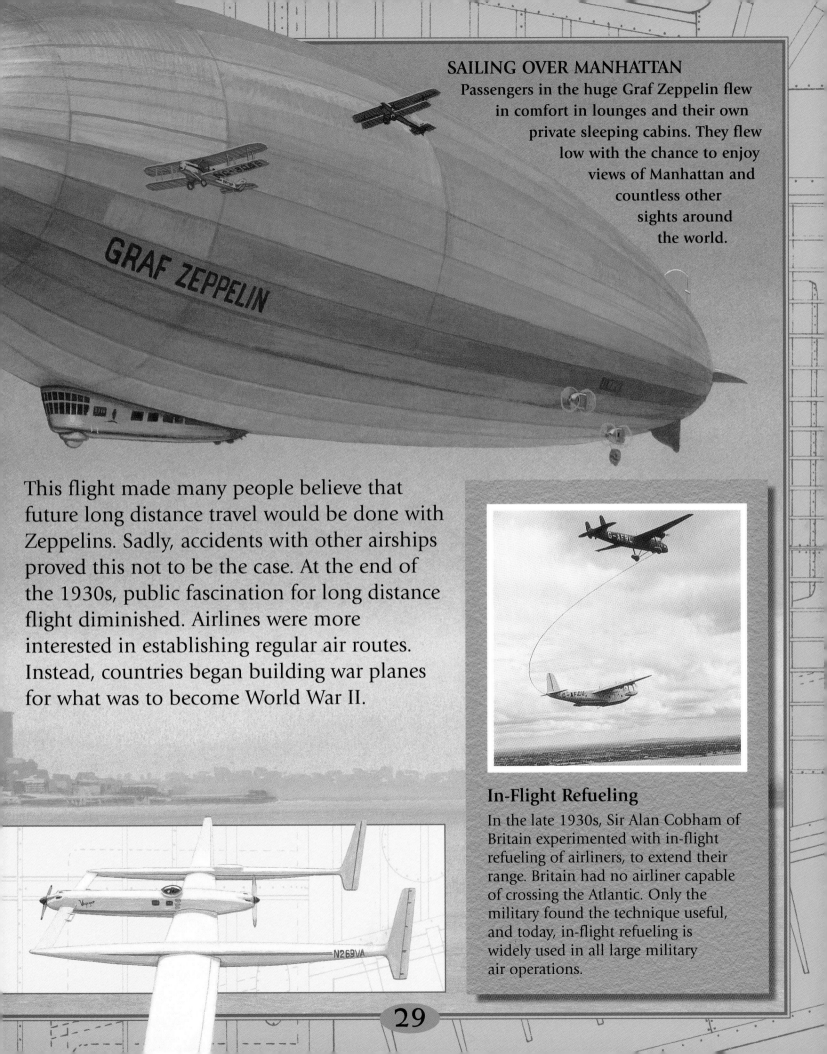

SAILING OVER MANHATTAN

Passengers in the huge Graf Zeppelin flew in comfort in lounges and their own private sleeping cabins. They flew low with the chance to enjoy views of Manhattan and countless other sights around the world.

This flight made many people believe that future long distance travel would be done with Zeppelins. Sadly, accidents with other airships proved this not to be the case. At the end of the 1930s, public fascination for long distance flight diminished. Airlines were more interested in establishing regular air routes. Instead, countries began building war planes for what was to become World War II.

In-Flight Refueling

In the late 1930s, Sir Alan Cobham of Britain experimented with in-flight refueling of airliners, to extend their range. Britain had no airliner capable of crossing the Atlantic. Only the military found the technique useful, and today, in-flight refueling is widely used in all large military air operations.

SPOTTERS' GUIDE

Aviators used very different aircraft on their epic flights. Some, like the Fokker VII and Ford Tri-motor, were among the best aircraft of their day. Others were less suited to long distance flying, but pilots used them because they could afford them. Engines became more reliable all the time. This was an important reason why pilots could set out on long and dangerous record-breaking flights.

ALCOCK AND BROWN
VICKERS VIMY
Length: 41 ft (12.5 m)
Wingspan: 68 ft 1 in (20.8 m)
Speed: 103 mph (166 km/h)

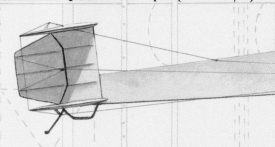

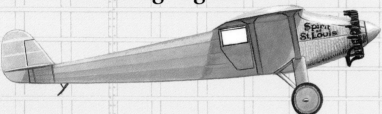

SPIRIT OF ST. LOUIS
RYAN NYP
Length: 27 ft 8 in (8.4 m)
Wingspan: 46 ft (14 m)
Speed: 124 mph (200 km/h)

WINNIE MAE
LOCKHEED VEGA
Length: 27 ft 6 in (8.4 m)
Wingspan: 41 ft (12.5 m)
Speed: 170 mph (274 km/h)

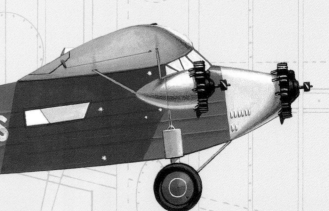

JASON
DE HAVILLAND DH 60
GYPSY MOTH
Length: 23 ft 6 in (7.2 m)
Wingspan: 30 ft (9.1 m)
Speed: 95 mph (153 km/h)

SOUTHERN CROSS
FOKKER F.VII-3M
Length: 47 ft 11 in (14.6 m)
Wingspan: 63 ft 4 in (19.3 m)
Speed: 118 mph (190 km/h)

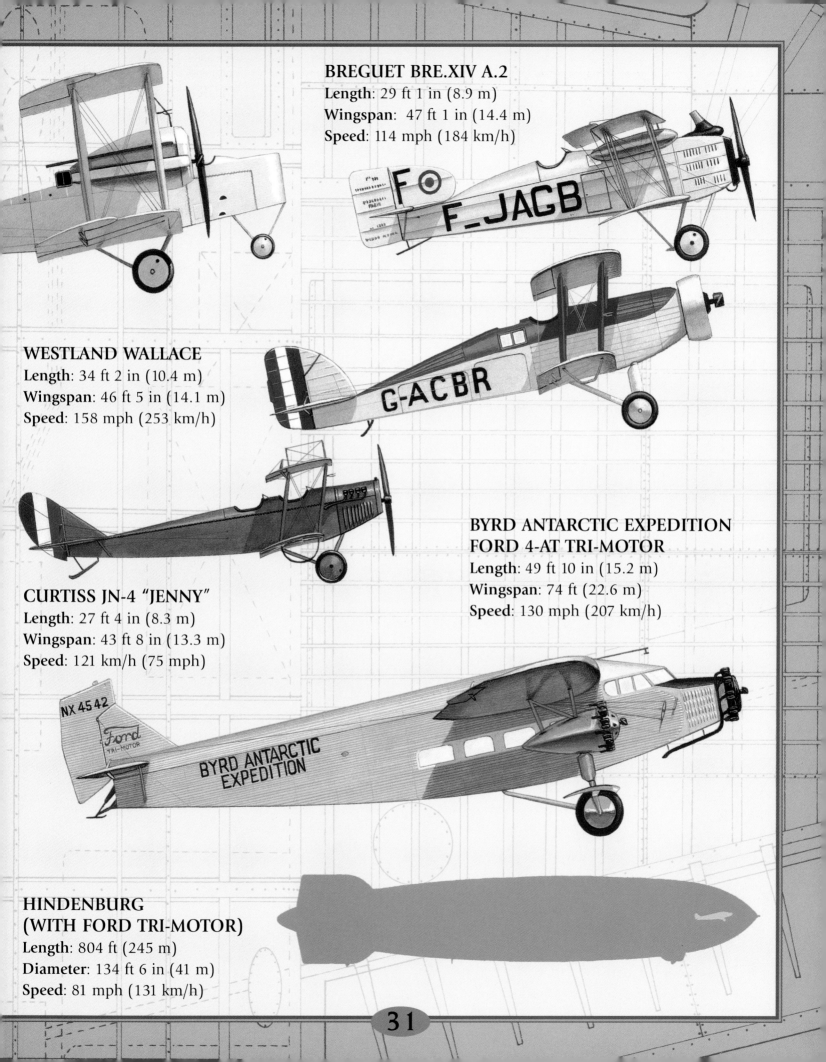

BREGUET BRE.XIV A.2
Length: 29 ft 1 in (8.9 m)
Wingspan: 47 ft 1 in (14.4 m)
Speed: 114 mph (184 km/h)

WESTLAND WALLACE
Length: 34 ft 2 in (10.4 m)
Wingspan: 46 ft 5 in (14.1 m)
Speed: 158 mph (253 km/h)

BYRD ANTARCTIC EXPEDITION
FORD 4-AT TRI-MOTOR
Length: 49 ft 10 in (15.2 m)
Wingspan: 74 ft (22.6 m)
Speed: 130 mph (207 km/h)

CURTISS JN-4 "JENNY"
Length: 27 ft 4 in (8.3 m)
Wingspan: 43 ft 8 in (13.3 m)
Speed: 121 km/h (75 mph)

HINDENBURG
(WITH FORD TRI-MOTOR)
Length: 804 ft (245 m)
Diameter: 134 ft 6 in (41 m)
Speed: 81 mph (131 km/h)

INDEX

GLOSSARY

AIR PRESSURE The pushing force of air.

AIRSHIP A self-propelled aircraft filled with a lighter-than-air gas.

ALTITUDE A height measured from sea level, or the Earth's surface.

AUTOGIRO An aircraft supported by a rotor instead of wings. The rotor spins itself and provides lift.

BIPLANE An aircraft that has two sets of wings.

BOMBER A plane used by the military to carry and drop bombs.

CENTER OF GRAVITY The point where all the weight of an object balances.

EXHAUST PIPE The pipe through which the waste gases escape from an engine.

FUEL INDICATOR An instrument that shows the amount of fuel left in the tank.

FUSELAGE The body of an airplane.

HEADWIND A wind that blows from directly in front.

IN-FLIGHT REFUELING The technique of refueling an aircraft while in the air.

NOBLEWOMAN A woman belonging to a high-ranking social class.

PERISCOPE An optical device made up of a tube and mirrors that allows a person to see objects that would otherwise be blocked.

SLIPSTREAM A current of air driven back by a spinning propeller.

SURPLUS An amount greater than what is needed.

TURBULENCE Stormy air caused by an air current moving against the flow of the main current.

UNDERCARRIAGE The landing gear of an aircraft.